MW01136510

The Rainbow Bee

By: Ricardo Gattas-Moras & Rob Jackson

By: Ricardo Gattas-Moras
& Rob Jackson

Copyright © 2020 by Ricardo Gattas-Moras
& Rob Jackson

All rights reserved. No part of this publication may be
reproduced, distributed, or transmitted in any form or by any
means, including photocopying, recording, or other electronic or
mechanical methods, without the prior written permission of the
publisher, except in the case of brief quotations embodied in
critical reviews and certain other noncommercial uses
permitted by copyright law.

Library of Congress Control Number: 2021926062

Authors' Quote:

"This is a book of love and acceptance. A reminder that our differences make us beautiful and special."

Once upon a time, in a beehive far away, a little bee was born who looked different than any other bee that had ever been seen. Instead of black and yellow, this bee had stripes that were all different colors, so the Queen decided to name the bee Rainbow.

Rainbow not only looked different, but liked different things too. Most of the hive prefered sweet nectar from garden flowers, however Rainbow's favorite was sour nectar from wild flowers.

But some bees thought Rainbow was too
different to be a part of the hive, so the
Queen decided to test Rainbow.

She asked to see if Rainbow could fly like
the other bees. Rainbow kept up with ease!
Also, positioning Rainbow at the front of the
swarm made it easier for the other bees
to follow along.

She asked to see if Rainbow could pollinate
flowers like the other bees. Rainbow was able
to pollinate perfectly, and could also pollinate
the flowers with sour nectar the other
bees didn't like.

She asked to see if Rainbow could buzz like the other bees. Rainbow flew around in circles and blissfully buzzed just like the others.

The tests made the hive realize that despite being unique and different, Rainbow still fit in great! The bees that doubted Rainbow apologized for not giving Rainbow a fair chance.

The Queen addressed the hive: "We're all a little different; Some taller, some shorter, some wider, some slimmer, some yellow and black, and some rainbow. But inside we're all the same."

"From now on, no matter what color or how different one of us is, we're going to love them all the same. Because it isn't our differences and the way we look that define us, it's how we act and treat others that determines our worth."

"**L**et's all remember that there is more that brings us together than separates us. So bee kind and bee open to others that are different, because loving someone is the best gift you can give to them and to yourself."

Rainbow looked up and smiled at the Queen
as the other bees gathered around to give
Rainbow hugs. From that day forward, the hive
loved and embraced one another's differences.
And Rainbow lived happily, and uniquely,
ever after.

The

Thank you to everyone who helped us along the way in turning this dream into a reality. A special thank you to our friends and family who have given us invaluable feedback, as well as unwavering love and support throughout this process. And most of all, thank you to our son, Cy, who's love for books at an early age inspired us to take this journey.

-Ricardo & Rob

Made in the USA
Middletown, DE
18 April 2023

29069276R00018